Managing Change with Personal Resilience

21 KEYS FOR BOUNCING BACK & STAYING ON TOP IN TURBULENT ORGANIZATIONS

Linda L. Hoopes

Dara Press

Atlanta, Georgia

Copyright © 2021 by Linda L. Hoopes, Ph.D.

All rights reserved. No part of this publication may be reproduced, distributed or transmitted in any form or by any means, including photocopying, recording, or other electronic or mechanical methods, without the prior written permission of the publisher, except in the case of brief quotations embodied in critical reviews and certain other noncommercial uses permitted by copyright law.

Dara Press
315 W. Ponce de Leon Ave., Suite 750
Decatur, GA 30030

www.darapress.com

Book Layout ©2017 BookDesignTemplates.com

Quantity sales. Special discounts are available on quantity purchases by corporations, associations, and others. For details, contact the "Special Sales Department" at the address above.

Managing Change with Personal Resilience: 21 Keys for Bouncing Back & Staying on Top in Turbulent Organizations/ Linda L. Hoopes, Ph.D.. —2nd ed.

ISBN 978-0-9987817-1-6

Contents

Author's Note iv

Foreword v

Part 1: Adapting to Change 1

1. Here Comes More Change 2
2. Why Change is So Challenging 7
3. Bouncing Back with Resilience 10
4. What is Your Change Quota? 15
5. Regaining Control 20
6. Anticipation is a Double-Edged Sword 23
7. Get Ready for Resistance 26
8. Are You Type D or Type O 30

Part 2: Seven Facets of Resilience 35

9. The Resilience Characteristics 36
10. Positivity 41
11. Confidence 45
12. Priorities 49
13. Creativity 53

i

14. Connection 56

15. Structure 59

16. Experimenting 62

Part 3: Enhancing Resilience 65

17. Developing Balance 66

18. Building a Resilience Development Plan 72

19. Resilient Teams 77

20. Working in a Nimble Organization 82

21. Living a Resilient Life 88

The 21 Keys 92

Resilience Reading List 96

About the Author 100

To Mark Kelly, with gratitude for getting me started on the authorship path.

Linda L. Hoopes

Author's Note

THIS BOOK WAS ORIGINALLY PUBLISHED in 2003. In this second edition, I have updated key terms (particularly around the labels given to the seven resilience characteristics) to be consistent with the terminology I am currently using. The rest of the content, including the foreword by Daryl Conner, has received minor updates. Although my thinking on resilience has continued to expand and evolve, I believe this book is still relevant and useful to people going through organizational change.

You can find additional perspectives and materials on resilience and change in my second book, *Prosilience: Building Your Resilience for a Turbulent World* (2017, Dara Press), and on these websites:
prosilience.com
realizationinstitute.com
resiliencealliance.com

Foreword

WE LIVE IN TURBULENT TIMES. We all know that life has become more hectic and confusing than we ever bargained for. But because we're in the churn every day, it's easy to lose perspective about what it all means.

When turbulence is the norm and pools of tranquility are all but a distant memory, an interesting paradox is formed. Unanticipated events and consequences become so prevalent that even those who have learned to "expect the unexpected" can't seem to escape the burden perpetual unrest imposes.

People absorb ambiguity and uncertainty at ever-increasing rates. Still, chaos regularly exceeds the last threshold they learned to accommodate, forcing yet another recalibration of expectations. This is true in all aspects of our lives, but seldom is it felt more profoundly than in the organizations where we spend so much of our time and energy.

In today's business environment, continuous, overlapping change has become a way of life, yet many of us feel progressively less prepared to resolve the problems and exploit the opportunities the gyrations produce.

When embarking on major new endeavors, organizations must find connecting links between the executives, managers, and employees affected by change initiatives. These links serve as the circuitry through which the energy of successful implementation flows. There are many such connections that can be formed; this book is about one of the more powerful ones.

Fostering a specific type of strength and flexibility dramatically increases the likelihood of achieving our desired goals, especially among individuals and teams feeling the impact of major disruptions. The single most important characteristic common among people who successfully navigate unfamiliar territory is what will be discussed here as "resilience."

A resilient person or team not only survives change but actually bounces back, stronger than before the challenge. Beyond making sound decisions about what to shift, developing personal and team resilience is the single most important task related to increasing an organization's competitive advantage during turbulent times.

Resilience is important at three levels in the organization—the individual, the team, and the enterprise as a whole. We must cultivate resilient individuals who can create and serve in resilient teams. These teams, in turn, need to function in the aggregate as "nimble" companies.

Resilience is the essential component that helps transform the mystery of change into a manageable process. In a world where up to two-thirds of all change efforts are considered failures (or partial successes at best), the degree of resilience demonstrated is what separates those who succeed from those who don't.

I can predict one thing with confidence—the number, sophistication, and pace of the changes headed your way will accelerate for the rest of your life.

Think of managing change as a generic life skill that you simply must possess. It is a general aptitude that allows you to survive and prosper in a world where the volume, speed, and complexity of change advance every year. Without this skill, the quality of existence (and possibly existence itself) can be in jeopardy. Resilience is one of the essentials to gaining mastery in this area.

For over three decades, I've attempted to better understand the role resilience has in the success of organizational change. Linda has distilled the critical findings from that work into 21 essential keys to help you better anticipate, understand, absorb, and adapt to the changes you and your organization will face in the coming years. In fact, she has uncovered and amplified insights far beyond any of my contributions.

Some of these principles and strategies she describes may seem like applied common sense. Others may come across as subtler in nature, while still others may seem counter-intuitive. Regardless of appearances, each of the 21 foundations presented here is based on years of solid observation and research involving thousands of people in hundreds of organizations.

I know you will enjoy this book, but I invite you to go beyond merely "reading" its contents. For maximum value, seriously invest yourself in what Linda has made available. Explore the potential for not only strengthening your own personal resilience, but the resilience of others close to you, the work team you rely on, as well as the resilience of your entire enterprise.

—Daryl R. Conner

Linda L. Hoopes

PART 1

Adapting to Change

"There is a river flowing now very fast. It is so great and swift that there are those who will be afraid. They will try to hold on to the shore. They will feel they are being torn apart and will suffer greatly.

Know the river has its destination. The elders say we must let go of the shore, push off into the middle of the river, keep our eyes open, and our heads above the water."

— Hopi Elders
Hopi Nation

CHAPTER 1

Here Comes More Change

Key #1: Recognize that change is here to stay.

The New World of Constant Change

WE LIVE IN A WORLD THAT IS CHANGING RAPIDLY. Managing the many changes in your life has become one of the most important tasks you face. The amount of change is increasing exponentially. The speed of change is accelerating. The complexity of change is expanding. The gap between changes is evaporating. Constant change has become a never-ending, overlapping, mind-boggling force in virtually everyone's lives.

Some of the driving forces creating change on a global scale include:
- the growth in the worldwide population;
- the globalization of the world economy; and
- the explosion of information.

These driving forces will shape our world and the direction it takes. You are not going to alter these things; instead, you must adapt to them.

If you work in an organization, you are almost certainly involved in a host of major changes, such as:
- mergers, acquisitions, and reorganizations;
- major new information systems;
- new jobs, new bosses, and new teams;
- challenging goals and aggressive plans; and
- new ways of doing business.

Understanding, assimilating, and adapting to the onslaught of changes has become business as usual in most organizations.

On top of these are even more changes that may be affecting your personal life, such as:

marriage, divorce, or a death in the family;
- kids, stepfamilies, teenagers, or seniors at home;
- a new home, new city, or new country; and
- new friends, acquaintances, and networks.
- And they just keep coming.

Our Reluctance to Change

We are not very good at adapting to this accelerated pace of change. Consider these dismal statistics[1]:
- More than half of the change initiatives by *Fortune 500* companies are unsuccessful. (*Why Systems Fail,* W. Schiemann, 1992.)
- More than half of major restructuring and reengineering projects fail. (*Reengineering the Corporation,* M. Hammer and J. Champy, 1994.)
- More than two-thirds of Total Quality Management projects fail.

---

[1] I realize these statistics are somewhat dated. However, a quick scan of recent research suggests that it is still accurate to say that a large proportion of change initiatives do not deliver the hoped-for results.

- More than 70% of mergers and acquisitions have failed to create any "synergistic value." (ICM Conferences, Inc., 1996.)
- More than 90% of information technology projects in large corporations fail. (The Standish Group.)
- More than half of marriages end in divorce.
- Most New Year's resolutions are never kept.

This is a lousy record. If you work in an organization, the chances are less than 50-50 that any major change will be successfully implemented. And the chances are less than 50-50 that your single most important relationship will survive. What is going on?

A lot of research has been conducted over the last 20+ years on this issue. In study after study, the primary cause for failure can be traced to the inability and resistance of people to make the necessary changes. It is not hardware, software, processes, or machines that cause the changes to fail. It's the people side of the equation.

You Are the Critical Ingredient

I believe that you as an individual are the single most important ingredient in determining whether change is successful or not. At its core, managing change is an individual issue, and successful change depends on whether you as an individual can adapt, and whether a critical mass of individuals in an organization can adapt together.

What most people lack is an understanding of how change affects them and what they can do to better anticipate and adapt to changes that come their way.

In addition to understanding the phenomenon of change, you also need some tools to help you survive and cope with the never-ending deluge of changes. This book will help give you an expanded perspective on dealing with change and the essential tools for navigating through turbulent waters.

Kayaking Down the River of Change

Think of change as a rushing river. That river has a natural course and flow. Now think of yourself as riding a kayak down the river. The currents are going to take you downstream whether you like it or not, but you have some choices about the ride. You can paddle or glide. You can maneuver around fallen trees near the banks or take your chances down the middle. You can go through the whitewater rapids, or pull the kayak out and try to walk around them. The river is always flowing, but you can choose how to navigate it.

Life is a river of change. But you have choices as to how you will negotiate the inevitable obstacles (changes) as they occur:
- You can resist and fight them.
- You can accept them and learn to live with them.
- You can adapt to them.
- You can initiate your own changes.

Going with the Flow

Mother Nature has shaped us to have two basic responses to changes that we perceive as threats. One is to stand and fight and try to conquer the threat. The other is to flee and get as far away as we can from it. Fight or flight. That's how we are wired.

In a 21st century world, neither option is very effective. Fleeing one change will only lead you into several more. And the likelihood of winning in a fight against some of the changes we are seeing in the world is extremely small. You need a third alternative to "fight or flight."

I call that third way "going with the flow." Going with the flow means that:
- you recognize that the river is the only way to get where you're going, and then . . .
- you plan a strategy for negotiating the river;
- you anticipate potential obstacles along the way;
- you remain open to unexpected twists and turns;
- you do what's needed to stay afloat—sometimes you paddle like crazy, other times you relax and let the river carry you; and
- you master the skills for adapting to change.

To be able to go with the flow most effectively, your most important asset is the quality of *resilience*. Resilience is the ability to bounce back from setbacks and keep going toward your goal even more effectively than before. In this book I have identified 21 key principles and strategies to help you increase your resilience so that you can get better at going with the flow. Some of these keys will help you understand and make sense of the changes swirling around you. Others will help you adapt to and manage the changes more effectively.

All of them will help you stay afloat and keep paddling with the current. So grab your paddle and let's head for the river.

Key #1: Recognize that change is here to stay.

Question for Reflection: Do you believe that change is here to stay, or have you convinced yourself that you're just one major change away from tranquility?

CHAPTER 2

Why Change is So Challenging

Key #2: Understand that loss of control is at the heart of change.

The Search for Control

ALTHOUGH WE DON'T ALWAYS LIKE TO ADMIT IT, humans seek control. Sometimes we are able to gain *direct* control—that is, we are in a position to choose what happens to us. Sometimes we have to settle for *indirect* control—we can at least see what's going to happen even if we don't like it. When neither one of these is available, we feel very uncomfortable.

Humans are also very smart. We are able to use our past experiences to establish *expectations* about how things in our lives are likely to unfold. These expectations provide a sense of control.

Change is challenging precisely because it disrupts our expectations—it creates a new reality that doesn't match the expectations we have created. This causes us to feel a loss of control. We sometimes exert a lot of effort to try to get the world to match our expectations. When that doesn't work, we try to establish expectations that match the new reality. This, however, takes energy.

Your Adaptation Budget

Adaptation is the process we use to adjust to the positive or negative implications of a major shift in our expectations. *Adapting to* or *assimilating* change is costly because it requires personal resources to make the shift. The resources we use include mental energy (to unlearn old ways of doing things and learn new ones), emotional energy (to work with our feelings and reactions), and physical energy (to engage in new behaviors).

Everyone has a certain capacity available for adapting to change. Some have more than others, but no one has an unlimited adaptation capacity. Think of your capacity as a "bank account" of points that you can use to pay for changes that take place in your life.

Each change that you encounter or initiate will cost you a certain number of points based on how much it disrupts your expectations; when you run out, your ability to adapt is limited. Let's explore this idea further.

The Price of Change

All changes, both major and minor, have an adaptation price tag attached. Everything counts, whether they are personal changes, family changes, or changes at work. The less the change matches what you expected to happen, the more resources you consume. And you will use up adaptation capacity whether you accept or reject changes that come your way.

Changes eat up capacity whether you initiate them or others impose them. Conventional wisdom says that if a change was your idea, it's easy (that is, it won't use much adaptation capacity). While this is partially true, some of the strongest resistance occurs when we get exactly what we wish for, if what we asked for causes a significant departure from our expectations.

For example, you may want to change jobs and end up finding one in another city. This leads you to sell your house, move your family, buy a new house, put the kids in new schools, adjust to new job demands, and learn to operate in a new organization. Although this is what you wanted, you must still deal with a host of unexpected problems and consequences of the new situation. And dealing with these changes uses up adaptation capacity.

Maximizing Your Adaptation Capacity

If you believe that each new year brings more change than the previous one, you can see the importance of continuously enhancing your ability to absorb new changes. This involves both increasing your adaptation capacity and learning how to reduce the level of resources demanded by each change.

The rest of this book focuses on the ideas and practices that will help you increase and manage your adaptation capacity. I will introduce you to the concept of *resilience*, and then focus in detail on the steps you can take to enhance your own performance during change.

Key #2: Understand that loss of control is at the heart of change

> **Questions for Reflection:** In what parts of your life do you experience the most control? The least?

Linda L. Hoopes

CHAPTER 3

Bouncing Back with Resilience

Key #3: Understand the importance of resilience in adapting to change.

What is Resilience?

PEOPLE WHO SUCCESSFULLY ADAPT to change tend to display a particular set of emotions, behaviors, and approaches. Although individuals in different countries demonstrate a range of cultural variations in the specifics of how they respond to change, the basic human processes of adaptation are essentially the same throughout the world.

By viewing change as a phenomenon that has a distinct shape and character, and by studying individuals and organizations that manage change effectively, you can learn to do things that are characteristic of those who manage change well. Instead of viewing change as a mysterious event, you can approach it as a process that can be understood and managed.

Of all the factors that contribute to adapting to change, the single most important factor is the degree to which individuals demonstrate *resilience*—the capacity to absorb high levels of change and maintain their levels of performance. The agility that resilient people show in the face of adversity results from having a certain elasticity that allows them to remain relatively calm in unpredictable environments. They can spring back repeatedly after being subjected to the disruption of change. In fact, when resilient people face ambiguity, anxiety, and a loss of control that accompany change, they tend to grow stronger from their experiences rather than feel depleted by them.

Resilient people face the same fear and apprehension as everyone else when they engage change. They are no less susceptible to change-related stress, but they are able to maintain their effectiveness as well as their physical and emotional stability while achieving most of their objectives. They face no less challenge than others when confronting a crisis, but they typically regain their equilibrium faster.

To continue our analogy, if you are kayaking down the river and hit a patch of whitewater that flips the kayak over so that your head is under water, resilience is the ability to "right yourself" faster, popping back up with less effort, so that you continue paddling with a minimum of disruption and loss of energy.

Resilience in Action

Imagine that you are a member of a small project team in a department of several teams. The company has just announced a reorganization. Your job and your team have been eliminated. All the team members will either have to find another job within the company or leave.

Another job has recently opened up, but it is in another department and another city. Your boss is strongly suggesting that you consider it. If you don't take it, you will probably have to leave the company, which you do not want to do.

At lunch with your team, you begin discussing the options for everyone. Several members give their reactions to the upcoming changes, but two of them, Jim and Kate, catch your attention.

Jim has been in the same role with the company since its founding. This was a source of pride for Jim but is now a handicap in his mind. He expresses his concerns:

Why did they have to change strategies? The way we were going was fine. I was here at the beginning, when there was just a small group of us. We got by on a shoestring budget. But now, with all these new products and new people, I think the company has bitten off more than it can chew.

Now they are talking about sending me halfway across the country—in a whole different job. They know I'm not going to do that. Being a systems analyst is all I've ever done. It's what I know and what I'm good at. Besides, they know my wife would never go for that. They must want me to quit. That merger has been a real disaster.

Kate, your project team leader for the last six months, has been with the company for several years, working on two or three teams, in a variety of roles. She stepped in as team leader midway through the project when things were in trouble. You had to admit she did a good job of getting everyone moving in the same direction and making progress in the critical areas that counted. What catches your attention is how different her perspective is from Jim's. Kate responds to Jim:

Jim, I'm sorry you feel that way. I guess I see the situation quite differently. Although I'm sorry to see this team break up, especially since we've been making such good progress, there are some new realities that we all are going to have to face up to, and some real opportunities in the situation.

First, our industry is changing, and things are going to get worse before they get better. We aren't the only ones in trouble,

and we are going to have to do some things differently if we are going to survive as a company.

Second, maybe the merger is not the perfect marriage that everyone seemed to think it would be. But it's given us some breathing space in our main markets, and an opportunity to grow into a new market that could potentially be bigger than any of the markets we now serve. I admit it's a risk, but it's a calculated bet that has a good chance of paying off big if we do it right.

We had a family conference last night at our house. I thought my family might be pretty resistant, but it didn't turn out that way at all. My husband is a chef and told me he sees this as his big chance to start his own restaurant. The kids were nervous at first, but we started searching the Internet for houses and activities in the area, and they started to get excited about it. So, to my surprise, they are pushing me to take the new job.

Jim, it sure couldn't hurt to at least go out and see what the company is offering. They will fly you and your family out there, drive you around the area, have you meet folks in the new department, and talk to someone in their relocation department. What have you got to lose? You might actually like it.

If you take the new job, you'll get an intensive two-month training program, followed by one-on-one coaching with one of the senior people in the department. If they didn't think you could do the job, they wouldn't have offered to make this kind of investment in you. I know it's new territory for you, but I think you would be a good fit. That's why I recommended you.

Resilience Makes the Difference

Here are two people in similar circumstances who see the same situation from fundamentally different angles. Why is that? I believe the difference is the quality of resilience. Kate's response is more resilient because it is likely to lead to quicker, more effective adaptation to the change than Jim's.

Now let's explore the factors that contribute to resilience and why it makes such a critical difference in times of change.

Key #3: Understand the importance of resilience in adapting to change.

Questions for Reflection: As you think about people you know, can you identify some who appear to be more resilient than others? What leads you to this conclusion?

CHAPTER 4

What is Your Change Quota?

Key #4: Know your quota for change.

Expectations and Perceptions

CHANGE MANAGEMENT IS basically about expectation and perception management. Two people look at the same change; one sees an exciting whitewater run, while the other sees certain disaster. When you can't control the change directly, two things that you *can* control are your expectations and your perceptions. Your initial view of a change affects how everything flows from that point on.

Your Capacity for Change

What is your tolerance level for change? Do you like no change, some change, or a lot of change? Where is your threshold? At what point do you say, "Stop! I just can't handle any more right now?"

As I mentioned earlier, "adapting to change" means using some of your adaptation capacity to recover from a significant disruption by developing new expectations that allow you to succeed in the unfamiliar environment.

It is possible for the demands of change to exceed your personal resources. One way to envision this is to imagine individual capacity as a sponge that can absorb a certain amount of liquid. As each change is poured into the sponge, it soaks in until the sponge becomes full. No matter how much additional change is poured in, the sponge cannot absorb any more, and the extra just rolls off.

Pouring more change into a "full sponge" can cause problems. When the oncoming "change load" exceeds your capacity for change, you may get upset and display dysfunctional behavior. What is that?

Dysfunctional Behavior

When we do not have the resources we need to set new expectations, we use our energy ineffectively, displaying a wide range of behaviors that do not contribute to our own well-being or that of our organization, family, or others. This dysfunction can show itself in a variety of ways, including:
- brief flashes of irritation;
- feeling stunned and numb;
- defensive behavior;
- psychosomatic illness;
- feelings of depression and despair; and
- errors and accidents.

The more out of control we feel, the more intense our negative reactions become.

Because dysfunctional behavior is costly, we are most effective when we live at a pace that allows us to take in and digest the changes we face without feeling that we are slipping out of control. At this pace, we can comfortably absorb and assimilate the changes around us without losing our equilibrium; we can live within our change quota.

Becoming aware of your own change quota is central to maintaining this sense of equilibrium. Knowing how much change you can comfortably handle lays the foundation for being able to deal with it as it arises.

Change Checklist

To begin sensitizing you to your change quota, review this list and check off any changes you are currently experiencing or are likely to experience soon.

Changes in Your Job

- ☐ You've changed jobs or have a new boss.
- ☐ You are working with a new team of people.
- ☐ You are using new tools, skills, or processes.
- ☐ You are working at a faster pace.
- ☐ You are working on a new project.

Changes within Your Organization

- ☐ A reorganization or merger has occurred recently.
- ☐ People have been laid off.
- ☐ Work processes are being redesigned.
- ☐ New information systems are being implemented.
- ☐ Your internal or external customer mix is changing.

Changes in Your Living Arrangements

- ☐ You are living with a different person or people.
- ☐ You're living in a new house or apartment.
- ☐ You've moved to a new neighborhood, city, or country.

Changes in Your Relationships

☐ You are recently married or divorced.
☐ You are dating a new person.
☐ You are meeting new friends or losing old friends.

Changes in Family Life

☐ New children/stepchildren have entered the picture.
☐ A child has moved away from home.
☐ A family member has recently died.
☐ Your spouse has started or stopped working outside the home.
☐ A family member is needing increased care.

Change in Life Circumstances

☐ You have become ill recently or overcome a major illness.
☐ You have become self-employed or started a new business.
☐ You are in the midst of changing your profession or career focus.
☐ You've experienced a major change in your financial situation—either positive or negative.
☐ You've changed your personal values, political beliefs, or spiritual orientation.
☐ Current events are affecting you at a personal level.

Other Changes

What other changes are you experiencing?

As you review this list and reflect on the changes you are currently dealing with, do you feel overwhelmed by all the changes or do you feel like you are taking them all in stride? This will be a pretty good indicator as to whether you are currently operating within your change quota.

Key #4: Know your quota for change.

> **Question for Reflection:** What are some of the signs and behaviors you notice in yourself when you start to exceed your change quota?

CHAPTER 5

Regaining Control

Key #5: Become more conscious of your own response to change.

Maintaining Equilibrium

BECAUSE THE ISSUE OF CONTROL IS SO CENTRAL to your reaction to change, let's review the process of regaining control. Understanding this process will enable you to see it in action—in yourself and in others.

You are hard-wired to try to make sense of the world—to seek balance between what you expect to experience, what you are actually experiencing, and your perceptions of the experience. You continuously try to make sure that what goes on in your environment is consistent with your expectations about how things should be.

A disruptive change is essentially a surprise—an experience that catches you off-guard. It is a situation where what you expected to happen and what happened do not match up in your mind. When that occurs, it triggers an automatic reaction as you struggle to adapt by coming to grips with the experience and making sense of what is happening to you.

Although the reaction is automatic and generally unconscious, you go through four main steps to sort through the experience and figure out how you should respond.

Step 1: You identify data as familiar or strange.

You are bombarded with a never-ending stream of data from your environment—what you see, hear, feel, and experience. As perceptions flow into your brain, the brain tries to match them with previous information stored in your mental "data bank." The first step in this process is to classify the data as familiar or unfamiliar.

If you recognize incoming perceptions as something familiar, you draw on your previous experience to make meaning of them. If you don't recognize the incoming data, and cannot retrieve a "match" from your data bank, your early warning indicators start to go off.

This triggers a second step.

Step 2: You make a judgment—a threat or not?

When you encounter strange data, your brain tries to make sense of it.

Based on eons of evolution, the primary sorting method is to determine whether or not the incoming data poses a potential danger. It is essentially a binary decision—friend or foe, opportunity or threat, benign or dangerous. If you do not classify the new experience as a threat, your warning indicators shut down. If, on the other hand, you cannot make sense of it, it is labeled a potential threat. You then try to determine how serious it is, how imminent the danger, and what could happen if you don't adapt in some way. If you determine that the threat is potentially serious, will happen soon, or will cause a lot of damage, you move on to the third step.

Step 3: You formulate a response.

The creation of a response to a potential threat is driven by the deeper need to maintain equilibrium. You need to formulate a plan of action to protect yourself from losing control.

You have two primary options. You can try to avoid the threat or you can seek to address and assimilate the change. If you choose to avoid it, you can try to pretend it doesn't exist (denial), or you can sidestep it (withdrawal).

If you choose to assimilate the change, your intention is to absorb the implications of the perceived threat and adapt to the consequences. You decide to confront the change, rather than trying to avoid it, by taking action that will allow you to reestablish the delicate balance between your expectations and your perceptions of reality. This leads to the fourth step.

Step 4: You adapt.

Finally, with plan in hand, you're ready to take action. You adjust and adapt as you just planned. You engage your response strategies and see if they work.

Success here means that equilibrium is restored and you reestablish a sense of control over your environment. However, it is not the old equilibrium that you went back and reclaimed. It is a new balance among what you now expect, what you experience, and how you perceive that experience. You have actually adapted to the change.

Key #5: Become more conscious of your own response to change.

> **Question for Reflection:** Think of a recent unexpected event that you experienced. Can you identify the process you went through to regain your equilibrium?

CHAPTER 6

Anticipation is a Double-Edged Sword

Key #6: Expect the unexpected so that you are rarely surprised that you are surprised.

A KEY SKILL FOR COPING WITH CHANGE is the ability to anticipate upcoming changes and their possible implications while leaving room for unanticipated consequences and contingencies. Let's focus for a moment on the expectations that underlie your response to change.

Your Expectations Drive You

What do you expect will happen tomorrow? What do you expect will happen next week? Where do you expect to be five years from now? What do you expect will happen with your spouse, your kids, your parents, your friends, your colleagues at work?

You are full of expectations. And they drive you. They allow you to predict and plan—you couldn't function without them.

Based on our previous experiences, we develop "mental models" about how things will unfold. These expectations may be positive or negative. They typically reflect not what you *want* to happen, but what you *believe* will happen. We take actions based on our expectations. When they are accurate, this works very well. But sometimes we're wrong. Our expectations are not correct. Things don't turn out as we thought they would.

This is especially likely in the midst of change. When things are in flux, our mental models don't work so well. As an example, think about driving your car. If you live in North America, you drive on the right-hand side of the road. But in traveling abroad, you may end up in a place where you need to drive on the left. Your unconscious expectations about which way to look before you turn, which side of the car you get in on, and a whole bunch of other things are just plain wrong. Even though you're doing something fairly familiar, you feel off-balance. Your mental models don't work so well.

This sense of being out of sync with the world is upsetting. When you get angry, it is often because something did not happen as you expected. Think of the last time you were frustrated, either at another person or in a specific situation. Now ask yourself: What expectation was not met? Did the other person not react as you thought they would, or should? Did this lead you to feel a loss of control?

The Double-Edged Sword of Anticipation

Being able to anticipate what's coming has tremendous benefits—if you're right! It allows you to prepare. It lets you stay in control so that you can respond effectively without getting angry or frustrated.

The downside of setting specific expectations, however, is that if you're wrong, you're setting yourself up for a fall. When reality fails to conform to your mental image, you become angry, frustrated, or disappointed because things didn't work out as you thought they should.

So, anticipation is a double-edged sword. If you didn't anticipate future events, you would lose your ability for even indirect control of a situation. Yet if you set specific expectations that prove to be inaccurate, you are defenseless against the loss of control that follows. What to do?

Expect the Unexpected

The answer to this dilemma is to learn to expect the unexpected. Develop the expectation that you will encounter surprises. That way, when you do, you won't get hit with a "double whammy." You'll be able to say, "Oh, yes. This is one of those surprises I was expecting."

The alternative, being surprised that you are surprised, is at the heart of feeling that the world around you is transforming faster than your own speed of change can accommodate. You will not be able to anticipate everything. There will be surprises along the way. The key is to accept future surprises as part of the equation and expect that some things will happen that you didn't foresee.

Plug the "X factor" of unknown events into your thinking, develop contingency plans with that "X factor" in mind, and be prepared to go with the flow of events.

Key #6: Expect the unexpected so that you are rarely surprised that you are surprised.

> **Question for Reflection:** In what ways have you factored the unexpected into your career planning?

CHAPTER 7

Get Ready for Resistance

Key #7: Be ready for resistance, whether you view a change as positive or negative.

Resistance is Normal

EXPERIENCING RESISTANCE IS A NATURAL part of any change process. Resistance at some level will occur with any significant shift in the status quo. You will tend to resist a major change whether you initially view it as a negative or positive turn of events. And there are predictable patterns that characterize resistance.

When your spouse complains about your sudden business trip or your child balks at a new babysitter, they are resisting change. When your colleagues argue about the merits of the new reorganization or complain about the time commitments to implement a new program at work, they are resisting change. Whenever something new or different is being introduced, there will be some level of resistance from those involved.

I've already discussed the reasons for resistance—we seek control, and change causes us to feel a loss of control. In

Managing at the Speed of Change, Daryl R. Conner describes the cycles of resistance that people experience. Now let's look at these predictable patterns of resistance.

Responses to Negatively Perceived Change

It comes as no surprise that you will tend to resist a change that you don't like. If you perceive a change as negative from the beginning—you don't want it but can't stop it—you will tend to pass through seven main stages:

1. **Immobilization:** You begin in a state of shock. ("What's happening to me?")
2. **Denial:** You reject the new information and refuse to absorb it. ("This can't be true.")
3. **Anger:** You become frustrated and often lash out in an attempt to fight back. ("I will get even.")
4. **Bargaining:** You begin negotiating and searching for some ground that helps to avoid the negative impact. ("What can I do to get out of this situation?")
5. **Depression:** You may become resigned to a failure to stop the negative impact, feel victimized, and become disengaged from your work. ("It's useless to try and fight back.")
6. **Testing:** You try and gain some sense of control by acknowledging the new limitations and exploring ways to redefine your goals and expectations. ("What can I do given my new constraints?")
7. **Acceptance:** You begin to accept and respond to the change realistically. This doesn't mean you like it, and you may accept the new reality grudgingly, but you come to the point where your expectations and reality are now realigned. ("I guess I can live with this. Perhaps I can try and make some lemonade out of lemons.")

This model is based on the work of Elisabeth Kübler-Ross, who studied people facing loss from terminal illness. While most negatively perceived changes are not this severe, we go through a similar cycle for any change that we experience as a loss.

Working through the negative response cycle can be expensive in terms of the time and emotional energy you will use. You may get stuck at one or more of the stages, resulting in some dysfunctional behavior. This can eat up an inordinate amount of assimilation points and may cause you to "blow your change quota." External assistance may help you move through this cycle.

Responses to Positively Perceived Change

Surprisingly, you will also tend to resist change that you perceive to be positive. Most people think that if they see a change as a good thing, they will tend to adapt with ease.

But that is not the case. As discussed earlier, even changes that are desired can disrupt our expectations. Marriage, a new job, buying a new house, winning the lottery—all have the potential for hidden surprises and loss of control. You will consume assimilation points and resist to some extent as you go through these five stages:

1. **Uninformed Optimism (Certainty):** You will experience an initial enthusiasm that is based on incomplete data. ("From what I hear, this change is going to be really good. It could save the company.")
2. **Informed Pessimism (Doubt):** You begin to doubt the wisdom of the change as you encounter unforeseen obstacles. ("When they first explained the new strategy, I didn't realize my job would change so much. I just don't think I can do it.")

If the pessimism overtakes your tolerance for doubt, you may withdraw from the change, or "check out." People sometimes check out publicly, declaring that they now see the change as negative, but sometimes they check out privately, pretending to be on board but really holding a negative view.

3. **Hopeful Realism (Hope):** Once you have worked through informed pessimism, you begin to have a more realistic understanding of the change and become more hopeful about being able to make the transition successfully. ("With some extra training and about three months to get used to the new system, I might just be able to do this.")
4. **Informed Optimism (Confidence):** As issues are resolved, you become increasingly confident that you will make it. ("This wasn't as hard to learn as I thought. My team is performing better than most of the others.")
5. **Completion (Satisfaction):** As you complete the change cycle, you become satisfied that it was worth the time and effort. ("With everything integrated into one system, things work a lot better. I didn't realize how primitive our previous system really was.")

Whether you initially perceive a change as positive or negative, it always comes with a price tag.

Key #7: Be ready for resistance, whether you view a change as positive or negative.

> **Questions for Reflection:** Think about the last major change that occurred in your life. Did you perceive it as positive or negative? In what ways did your responses follow the cycles described above?

CHAPTER 8

Are You Type D or Type O?

Key #8: Know your orientation to change—danger or opportunity.

Change is a Paradox

IT HAS BEEN SAID that the Chinese express the concept of crisis as a combination of two symbols, with one representing potential danger and the other conveying potential opportunity. Although there is some question about whether this is a correct interpretation of the Chinese symbols, the idea that change is a paradox containing both danger and opportunity is very powerful. Let's look at your orientation to change from these two perspectives.

Research suggests that some individuals have a "Type-D" orientation toward change, focusing primarily on the dangerous implications of unfamiliar situations, while others have a "Type-O" orientation, focusing on the promise of new opportunities. Most people fall between these two extremes, but for simplicity's sake I will describe the two ends of the continuum.

Type D (Danger Orientation)

Change is particularly difficult for Type-D people. Because they tend to focus on dangers, they are fairly quick to experience a loss of control. They find themselves overwhelmed by the demands of multiple changes. The resulting dysfunctional behavior, in turn, is an additional source of disruption for them, and so they can get into a spiral in which it is increasingly difficult for them to regain control during periods of change. Or they may defend against change as long as possible by denying or distorting data about situations that would require them to adapt.

The tendency to view change negatively also makes it more likely that Type-D people will find themselves in the cycle of resistance to negatively perceived change, dealing with emotions such as anger, denial, and depression, which consume high levels of resources. In short, Type-D people have a strong preference for stability and lack many of the skills needed to move themselves through the process of adaptation.

The Type-D orientation to change is not limited to individuals. Families, teams, and whole organizations can take on a "danger" orientation during change, limiting their potential to effectively adjust to new circumstances. If you are in a group or organization that displays a Type-D orientation, you may find that this way of thinking is contagious, leading you to see change more negatively than you otherwise might.

Type O (Opportunity Orientation)

By contrast, Type-O people move more easily through the challenge of change. Because they start with the view that change is an opportunity from which they can benefit, they are often excited, rather than frightened, when disruption occurs. It typically takes a larger disruptive force to cause them to feel out of control than it does their Type-D counterparts, primarily because their expectations encompass a wide range of possibilities, both negative and positive. They are not immune to disruption and loss of control, but when they do experience these things they are able to recover quickly and move on.

Type-O people do experience resistance when their expectations are disrupted, but their tendency to see opportunities may make it more likely that they will begin with an initially positive perception and then hit the "informed pessimism" form of resistance. If they come through to the "informed optimism" side of the cycle, they have an increased sense of possibility that shapes how they view future change.

What's Your Orientation?

Most people are a mixture of Type D and Type O. As you think about your history of change, you can probably think of situations in which you have displayed each of these orientations. However, there is probably one of the orientations that characterizes you somewhat better than the other. Do you tend to see change as a dangerous threat or as a new opportunity? Do you react to change with fear and denial, or do you embrace change and move quickly to adapt to the new opportunity?

These are not questions that others can answer for you. You can get feedback from colleagues, friends, or family, which may give you some insights. But, in the end, you have to honestly assess for yourself into which category you fall.

What Makes the Difference?

This leads, of course, to the obvious question: Where do these orientations come from? How do we become Type-D or

Type-O? Research suggests that our orientations are shaped very early in life—some theorists even suggest that we are born with them. I believe that your orientation reflects early influences—your parents, other important individuals, experiences with success or failure in change—combined with what you have learned throughout your life. I also believe that you can learn new lessons about the perspectives and skills that will move you toward the Type-O end of the continuum. The remainder of this book describes the perspectives and characteristics shared by Type-O individuals and will guide you in moving toward greater resilience.

Key #8: Know your orientation to change—danger or opportunity.

Question for Reflection: Where did you learn your orientation toward change?

PART 2

Seven Facets of Resilience

*"Our greatest glory is
not in never falling,
but in rising
every time we fall."*

—Confucius

Linda L. Hoopes

CHAPTER 9

The Resilience Characteristics

Key #9: Understand the elements of resilience.

Your Speed of Change

YOU HAVE A PERSONAL SPEED OF CHANGE. Your speed of change is the rate at which you move through the adaptation process with a minimum of unproductive behavior. It is the pace at which you can bounce back from the confusion caused by uncertainty and grasp the opportunities that a new environment presents.

The single most important factor for enhancing this speed of change is *resilience*. Resilient individuals—those who can operate at a high speed of change—have a distinct advantage. They are able to take on more change and maintain or enhance their performance without becoming so intellectually, physically, and emotionally drained by the experience.

Maintaining your equilibrium requires that you practice certain resilient "habits of mind." These habits allow you to maximize your ability to absorb change and continue to perform effectively. They are the critical ingredients for being able to bounce back quickly and stay on top. Our research points to seven facets of resilience that help you adapt to change.

The Seven Facets of Resilience

Based on a framework originally presented in Daryl Conner's *Managing at the Speed of Change*, I have identified a set of seven core characteristics of resilient behavior:

1. **Positivity:** Effectively identifying opportunities in turbulent environments.
2. **Confidence:** Believing you have the capability to succeed during change.
3. **Priorities:** Having a clear vision of what you want to achieve and using it to guide yourself when disoriented.
4. **Creativity:** Opening up a range of options and possibilities for responding to change.
5. **Connection:** Drawing on the resources that others can provide during change.
6. **Structure:** Using processes and systems effectively to manage ambiguity during change.
7. **Experimenting:** Initiating action in the face of uncertainty, taking calculated risks rather than seeking the comfort of the status quo.

These seven facets of resilience prove to be the critical ingredients for being able to bounce back and adapt to change effectively.

The combination of these characteristics is quite powerful. Each attribute plays a role in protecting your adaptation resources during change. When they are balanced and used wisely, they create a strong force for effective transformation.

Each Characteristic is Important

Each of these seven facets of resilience is important by itself. Although they are interrelated, they represent separate and distinct aspects of a fully formed approach to change. Yet they are most effective when they are combined in action.

Collectively, they can be seen as reflecting the key components of effective problem-solving when encountering disruption.

Because each new challenge calls on a different constellation of resilience factors, the characteristics are not equally critical in every situation. For instance, an individual might run into a situation where the most important aspect of her response is the ability to be extremely creative and think of a wide range of possible actions. Another person might be in a situation where the ability to stay focused on his highest priorities is the most critical element. At various points in time, all the characteristics are important.

For this reason, it is impossible to say that there is a single "trait" called resilience. Instead, you should view resilience as the ability to draw on whichever characteristics, or combination of characteristics, is called for in a particular situation.

A Quick Self-Assessment

Read each item and check off your rating:

Compared to most people, I believe I apply this element of resilience:

	Much Less	Less	About the Same	More	Much More
1. *Positivity*—I view the world as complex but filled with opportunity. During disruption, I can see opportunities rather than just focusing on the problems and dangers in a situation.					
2. *Confidence*—I believe I am a valuable, capable person; I am confident in my ability to capitalize on opportunities. Regardless of the situation, I know I can find a way to succeed.					
3. *Priorities*—I have a clear vision of what I want to achieve, and a sense of purpose and focus in life. When things are turbulent, I can set clear priorities and stay focused on them.					
4. *Creativity*—I am open-minded and comfortable with paradoxes and ambiguity. When dealing with new situations, I gather information from a variety of perspectives and try varied approaches to problem-solving.					
5. *Connection*—I have strong social bonds and am comfortable in a variety of social situations. During change, I recognize my interdependence with others, and am able to call on others for support and assistance when necessary.					
6. *Structure*—When faced with an ambiguous problem or an unfamiliar situation, I quickly set about developing a structured approach to address it. I enjoy creating order out of chaos, and developing effective systems for organizing information.					
7. *Experimenting*—I enjoy trying new things and challenging myself. I explore unfamiliar situations rather than avoiding them. I will take action even when I am not sure what the outcome will be.					

Summary

If you think about these characteristics as a road map for solving problems and making decisions in new or uncertain situations, they can be summarized as follows:

- You start by engaging your energy in unfamiliar situations because you see opportunities (*Positivity*) and view yourself as capable of responding to them (*Confidence*).
- You then focus on what's important, targeting your efforts toward the most important elements (*Priorities*).
- You generate options in your own mind (*Creativity*) and by drawing on others (*Connection*).
- You organize those possibilities into a disciplined approach (*Structure*).
- Finally, you initiate action to try out your solutions despite uncertainty (*Experimenting*).

The next seven chapters of this book focus on the seven facets of resilience. I will describe each characteristic, show why it is critical, and provide some practical tips for strengthening your capability in that area.

In Part 3, I will explore how to achieve better balance among the characteristics and how to use them to your best advantage in teams, in organizations, and in your life.

Key #9: Understand the elements of resilience.

> **Question for Reflection:** When you think about people you know who appear to manage change effectively, in what ways can you observe them applying these characteristics?

CHAPTER 10

Positivity

Key #10: Look for the opportunities in changing situations.

Dangers and Opportunities

EACH PERSON WHO VIEWS a turbulent environment sees something different. And what a person sees often says more about them than about the situation. To a large degree, change is in the eye of the beholder.

In every change there are both dangers and opportunities. To ignore either of them is to run the risk of missing important information.

Resilient individuals do not overlook the dangers; however, they focus their primary attention on opportunities. They believe that the world presents a stream of possibilities, and they typically find good things in most unfamiliar situations. Unexpected events become a chance to explore new perspectives.

Indicators of Positivity

When you apply the *Positivity* characteristic, you will tend to:
- see the value in new opportunities;
- learn useful lessons from setbacks;
- look for the good in bad situations; and
- be generally upbeat about the future.

The strength of your positivity is a very good indicator of how much openness to new possibilities you have in your general operating style. The stronger this characteristic is, the less cautious you tend to be when opportunities present themselves.

For example, let's say your company is being reorganized, and your department may be decentralized or outsourced. With strong positivity, you may see the benefits of working in another department, gaining a wider scope in your new role, or ending up in a better position than you are now. You may believe that the opportunities you identify are worth taking some additional risk and energy to pursue, because your job is currently in jeopardy and because you believe it is possible to "land on your feet" if you take the chance to influence events.

Your world view, positive or negative, is an important element in whether you are a Type-O person (you see the opportunities) or Type D person (you see the dangers). If you are Type O, you will see an exciting whitewater run in the reorganization. If you are Type D, you will see a disaster in the making with the potential for you to capsize.

With low positivity, you might interpret the same scenario as "just another attempt to lay people off," see your department as a target, and believe that there's nothing you can do about it except hope it's not too bad. You would tend to not see any "silver linings in the clouds" or ways that your work life could actually be better.

When you see the world more negatively, the assumption you hold is that the status quo is probably better than any change would be, and that your situation could only get worse. You may tend to conclude that matters are out of your hands, and that it is not worth the personal resources or the risk to try and alter the situation.

How Does Positivity Protect Adaptation Capacity?

The ability to see opportunities in new situations makes it more likely that you will be in an optimistic mood. This, in turn, enables you to call on a larger supply of mental energy, and to use your adaptation capacity more effectively to address challenges.

When you don't demonstrate positivity, you are likely to spend your adaptation capacity in avoidance, worry, and rumination, rather than on finding solutions to the issues you are facing.

Becoming More Positive

Here are five practical things you can do to develop greater positivity:

1. Become more aware of the things you say to yourself when you encounter an unfamiliar situation. If possible, ask someone who knows you well to give you candid feedback on your ability to identify opportunities in new situations.
2. Think of a particular challenge you are currently facing. Identify specific ways in which this challenge could present opportunities for you.

3. Practice turning "minuses" into "pluses." Divide a sheet of paper in half vertically and list the negative factors related to a proposed change on one side. Then, write a positive statement to go with each negative factor. Ask yourself, "What can I do to make the negative factors positive?"
4. If you become frustrated or find yourself becoming negative about a new situation, take a "time-out" moment to step back. Once you have relaxed a bit, refocus your attention on the benefits and positive payoff of succeeding.
5. Pick a very positive person and ask them to coach you.

Key #10: Look for the opportunities in changing situations.

Questions for Reflection: At what times of the day is it easiest for you to see the world optimistically? Why? How can you carry this feeling into other parts of your day?

CHAPTER 11

Confidence

Key #11: Develop a "can-do" attitude.

Believing in Yourself

THE SECOND RESILIENCE CHARACTERISTIC is having confidence in yourself. *Confidence* includes your belief in yourself, your ability to assess your own capabilities, and your ability to weather setbacks.

People with a favorable view of themselves have a "can-do" attitude. They also have a sense of their own strengths and skills. They believe they can succeed in difficult situations and are willing to tolerate the occasional disappointment. This allows them to act decisively and persist in overcoming obstacles.

Indicators of Confidence

When you apply the *Confidence* characteristic, you will tend to:
- see yourself as a valuable, capable person;
- feel equipped to deal with whatever comes your way;
- not feel victimized by circumstances; and
- see your actions as influencing others and events.

By believing in yourself, you tend to interpret situations as providing opportunities for you to apply your skills. Your self-confidence gives you the foundation for constructively dealing with unfamiliar situations.

For example, let's stay with our reorganization example from the last chapter, and say that the main reason for the reorganization of your department is that a major company-wide computer information system is being installed. If your department is to be decentralized or outsourced, you might be offered another assignment working with new customers to help them link into your new system. You were not the first choice for this assignment because you lacked the computer skills, but management thought your people skills would be valuable in establishing good long-term customer relationships.

With a negative view of yourself, you might interpret this situation as the company picking you as a poor second choice. You would doubt your ability to learn the new system. You might see this as the company's way of setting you up to fail, forcing you to leave soon.

With a strong positive view of yourself, you might see this situation as an opportunity to "get closer to the customer" and be of increased value to your organization. Although you lack the computer skills right now to be effective, your confidence in your own ability to learn new things would help you see that you could quickly learn them in the classes being held over the next six months. And although you weren't the first choice, you believe in yourself and see this as an opportunity to show the company that they made the best choice after all.

How Does Confidence Protect Adaptation Capacity?

The belief that you can succeed despite uncertainty makes it more likely that you will apply your adaptation capacity in early problem-solving steps. The success gained from these steps can serve as fuel for the next, more difficult, phases of the process, providing more energy for you to use.

If you lack confidence in your abilities, you will tend to see the inevitable setbacks that occur in any change as evidence of your own lack of capability. This will tend to make you withdraw your adaptation capacity from problem-solving activities and use it up in protecting yourself.

Becoming More Confident

Here are five practical things you can do to develop greater confidence:

1. Take an inventory of your job-performance-related strengths and weaknesses and make a balanced assessment of your overall abilities.
2. Celebrate and reinforce specific achievements—a new job or promotion, graduation, learning something new, overcoming adversity.
3. Set aside time to develop a skill that you believe will be valuable to you in your work.
4. Imagine yourself at some future event celebrating your success. How did you get there? "Dream backwards" from that point in the future to the present. Figure out what you did to succeed and begin in the present to take the steps that will get you there.
5. Pick a person who values you and ask them to coach you.

Key #11: Develop a "can-do" attitude.

> **Questions for Reflection:** What information do you use to decide whether you feel good about yourself? Do you rely on others' evaluations, your own, or some combination?

CHAPTER 12

Priorities

Key #12: Keep your focus on long-term goals and values.

A Clear Sense of Purpose

RESILIENT INDIVIDUALS BRING a built-in sense of direction and clarity of purpose to their actions. Change of any kind tends to disrupt events, throw people off course, and introduce uncertainty into the equation. Without a means to sort and prioritize events, you can easily lose your way and waste your adaptation resources.

Resilient people have a well-defined set of values and goals built on an overall sense of direction. They rely on this sense of direction to guide their choices and set new priorities in the face of disruption.

The specific values that form this focus may vary from person to person. They may reflect a strong moral philosophy, a political ideology, a company vision, or some other set of core beliefs. Whatever their source, these values allow resilient individuals to sort through disruptive events, conserve their adaptation resources, and chart a path through the fog of change.

Indicators of Priorities

When you apply the *Priorities* characteristic, you will tend to:
- have long-term goals;
- be committed to achieving those goals;
- set priorities; and
- use those goals and priorities to guide everyday actions.

During times of change, you will be able to fall back and refocus on those long-term goals as you revise your priorities in the light of new circumstances.

For example, let's say that you were presented with the opportunity to move to another country for a two-year assignment. You would need to sell your house and move your family there as well. The assignment is challenging and the location is attractive, but when you returned, the job you left would no longer be there and you would be reassigned to another job that is not yet defined, or you would need to seek other global opportunities within the company.

Without a focus on long-term goals, you might treat this as a short-term decision and base your decision on short-term factors—the appeal of staying in your current job as long as possible, the potential disruption to your family in the next two years, and the uncertainty of your future job prospects.

However, with a long-term sense of purpose, you might see this opportunity very differently. You might view this as the chance of a lifetime for you and your family to experience another culture, to become global citizens, to expand your knowledge of the company's world-wide network, and position yourself for projects or jobs with much broader scope and impact.

How Do Priorities Protect Your Adaptation Capacity?

Change is characterized by high levels of ambiguity, making it difficult to know where to invest your adaptation capacity. Clear priorities will enable you to choose the one or two activities that will have the highest payoff for you and to say "no" to the rest, conserving your adaptation resources for the most important things.

If you lack clarity about your goals and purpose, you are likely to divide your attention across many possible actions. If you try to do everything at once, and have difficulty identifying and saying "no" to lower-priority activities, you will waste a lot of your resources.

Strengthening Your Priorities

Here are five practical things you can do to develop and apply clear priorities:

1. Spend some time identifying the things that are most important in your life. One way to do this is to write an imaginary future obituary for yourself. What would you want people to say was important in your life?
2. Look at your calendar for the past few weeks and see how much time you have spent on various types of activities. Evaluate whether you are spending your time focusing on the things that are most important to you.
3. Visualize yourself as you would like to be in five years. Identify one or two steps you could take now that will move you in that direction.
4. Think about a major change project in which you are currently involved and identify how its successful completion relates to your personal goals.
5. Identify a very focused person and ask them to coach you.

Key #12: Keep your focus on long-term goals and values.

> **Questions for Reflection:** How has your focus changed over the past five or ten years? What priorities have remained consistently important for you over that time?

CHAPTER 13

Creativity

Key #13: Generate a wide range of possibilities to creatively address uncertainty.

Strategies and Options

UNFAMILIAR SITUATIONS can rarely be conquered with familiar means. As obstacles are encountered, it is often necessary to repeatedly modify your strategies. Resilient individuals draw ideas and energy from internal and external sources.

Resilient people are creative. They can generate a wide range of thoughts and potential responses without feeling the need to decide on one response immediately. This conceptual flexibility is based on a tolerance for ambiguity (the ability to operate effectively in environments characterized by uncertainty) combined with an ability to think of many different approaches. The resulting wealth of possibilities provides a variety of strategies for attacking a problem.

In contrast, less-resilient people tend to see the world in "either/or" terms. They are very uncomfortable in uncertainty and seek sure answers when there may not be any. This desire for closure can sometimes get in the way during change.

Indicators of Creativity

When you apply the Creativity characteristic, you will tend to:
- enjoy new or complex ideas;
- tolerate ambiguity well;
- be open to different perspectives; and
- generate creative solutions for adapting to change.

Being a creative thinker helps you avoid "black and white" choices, allowing you to see the complexities and "shades of gray" in uncertain situations, and it increases the range of options you have available.

For example, imagine that you have completed a critical report and need to get it to a client by the end of the day, but your computer has crashed and you are not able to send it via e-mail as you had planned. High levels of creativity might enable you to scan your most recent printout and text it from your phone.

If you are not a creative thinker, however, you might tend to stick with familiar approaches that are much more costly, such as retyping the whole report on someone else's computer so that you can stick with your original plan of e-mailing it.

How Does Creativity Protect Adaptation Capacity?

Creative thinking is an important part of the brainstorming process. The more different possibilities you can come up with for how to deal with an unfamiliar situation, the more likely it is that one or more of the ideas will help you master the challenge.

If you find it difficult to break out of routine patterns of thinking, you may waste your adaptation capacity trying old approaches even though you know they won't work very well.

Becoming More Creative

Here are five practical things you can do to develop more creativity in your thinking:
1. Swap sides in a discussion on a topic you feel strongly about—argue your friend's or colleague's side and ask them to argue yours.
2. In the midst of change, learn to suspend your judgment. Don't assume that the first answer you come up with is the best or the only one.
3. Practice thinking of paradoxes (both/and) rather than contradictions (either/or). For instance, identify three positives *and* three negatives about a new idea or concept rather than focusing exclusively on one or the other.
4. Offer to work in a role that may be unfamiliar to you so that you can learn to see the world from a different point of view.
5. Find a person who is strong in creativity and ask them to coach you.

Key #13: Generate a wide range of possibilities to creatively address uncertainty.

> **Question for Reflection:** What people, places, or events provide you with sources of new insights, ideas, and possibilities?

Linda L. Hoopes

CHAPTER 14

Connection

Key #14: Reach out to others for perspective and support.

Developing Strong Connections

ANOTHER CONTRIBUTOR to the ability to generate options and possibilities is strong connections. Resilient people tend to draw on the resources of others. They supplement their own knowledge and skills with the talents of others. They realize that they do not have all the answers and that other people can often supply critical pieces to the puzzle. Without depending on others exclusively, they build effective networks for the free exchange of information and support.

People with a strong *Connection* characteristic tend to have a clear sense of their own strengths and weaknesses. As a result, they know when they need to reach out to others to help shore up a skill they may lack. They relate to others easily and find it natural to reach out for assistance during change without threatening their own self-concepts.

In contrast, some people prefer to "go it alone." When they are feeling uncertain, they retreat from others, either because they find it difficult or threatening to show an area of weakness, or because they believe that they can come up with more effective responses alone.

Indicators of Connection

When you apply the *Connection* characteristic, you will tend to:
- recognize where others can add value;
- appreciate the ideas of others;
- work well in a team setting; and
- draw on others for support.

Connection allows you to avoid the trap of seeing your own perspective as the only valid one. For example, if your company is planning a merger, and you are asked to design the plan for integrating the two computer systems, high levels of connection might lead you to call a couple of colleagues and acquaintances who have done similar projects and ask them for input. Then, once you have a draft of the plan, you might ask a trusted colleague to review it before finalizing. Someone with a low level of connection might attempt to design the plan without any external assistance and then turn it in without getting any additional review or input.

How Does Connection Protect Adaptation Capacity?

The broader the range of ideas and resources you can bring to a new situation, the stronger your solutions will be. Connection allows you to use your resources efficiently by focusing on the parts of the task where your unique contribution is most valuable and to draw on practical, emotional, and conceptual assistance from others to support you.

Low levels of connection can lead to resources wasted in "reinventing the wheel" and solutions that are not as good as they could be—and potentially to isolation and loneliness.

Building Connection

Here are five practical things you can do to develop your *Connection* characteristic:

1. Identify colleagues who have perspectives and ideas that are different from your own, and make it a point to ask their opinions when you are trying to solve a problem.
2. When a colleague comes to you with an idea that sounds crazy or stupid, step back and try to see it from their point of view before responding.
3. Ask friends or colleagues for their opinions on your thoughts about a change you are facing and listen to their answers without interrupting them or passing judgment on their ideas or suggestions.
4. Identify a skill you would like to learn and solicit the assistance of an individual who can teach it to you.
5. Find a person who is highly effective in connection and ask them to coach you.

Key #14: Reach out to others for perspective and support.

Questions for Reflection: Which people in your life do you turn to for emotional support? For practical assistance? For helping you define and refine your ideas?

CHAPTER 15

Structure

Key #15: Create systematic approaches to managing ambiguity.

Putting Things in Order

RESILIENT PEOPLE HAVE the ability to transform the confusion of ambiguous situations by applying structured approaches. When change occurs, an overwhelming amount of new data must be managed. In addition, there is a wide range of new possible strategies to consider.

It is crucial to be able to impose some logical structure on events, both internally and externally. Resilient individuals are able to categorize information, sequence elements into a plan, attend to the necessary details, and discipline themselves to take action using their newly formed tactical plans. In some cases, this ability to organize things takes on a physical dimension as well—arranging things so that they are efficiently and effectively used.

Resilient people are methodical in their approach, using appropriate models to sort and process the new stream of information. Without these structures in place, resources can be lost in confusion, miscommunication, and lack of coordination.

Indicators of Structure

When you apply the *Structure* characteristic, you will tend to:
- quickly sort information;
- identify patterns in new situations;
- build systems to manage chaos; and
- plan actions that maximize efficient use of resources.

While many people can structure things in a way that helps them personally, the most effective organizers also tend to create systems for managing information that are helpful to others. This becomes critical in turbulent organizations during times of change.

For example, imagine that your organization has decided to launch a new series of products, and your role is to develop creative, vivid descriptions of each product for potential customers, which is something you've never done before. Applying your skill in structure, you create a standard process for developing, editing, proofing, and storing the new descriptions. An individual with low levels of structure might focus their attention on the creative aspects of the task and fail to systematize the process in ways that could prove helpful.

How Does Structure Protect Your Adaptation Capacity?

This characteristic is easy to overlook. People sometimes underestimate the ways in which structure can be helpful during change. But, in fact, this characteristic plays a critical role. The ability to build systems, plans, and structures is essential to allowing people to coordinate their efforts during change.

In addition, structure enables effective use of resources by ensuring that tasks are sequenced appropriately, time is used wisely, and details attended to.

Low levels of structure can lead to wasted capacity by creating physical and psychological disorder, making it difficult to sequence activities, locate materials, and think through the consequences of specific actions.

Becoming Better at Structure

Here are five practical things you can do to improve your ability to create structure:

1. Use a day planner. Devote a separate section to each major area of your life. Keep track of commitments, plans, and next steps for each change initiative.
2. Identify the types of organizing structures and practices that work best for you. Figure out what helps you sort through confusing or unfamiliar situations.
3. Break down an ambiguous situation into smaller components. Look for both the opportunities and potential problems in each piece.
4. Make a to-do list for a change project. Start by clearly visualizing the desired outcomes. Work backwards from there and identify the major steps that will help you get there.
5. Find a person who has strong skills in applying structure and ask them to coach you.

Key #15: Create systematic approaches to managing ambiguity.

Question for Reflection: Can you identify some systems or processes that you have built into your life, in the form of daily routines, the way you perform specific activities, the layout of physical spaces, and other systematic things that you may not typically view as "structures"?

CHAPTER 16

Experimenting

Key #16: Try out new approaches and solutions.

Moving into Uncertainty

EFFECTIVE STRATEGIES FOR ADAPTING to change are only useful if they are applied when the time is ripe. As circumstances change, windows of opportunity open and close swiftly. The person who waits for complete certainty before taking action loses the chance to take advantage of favorable conditions.

The failure to capitalize on an opportunity can be extremely costly in two ways. First is the cost of the lost opportunity itself—what might have been. Second is the cost of the resources that are spent to build plans that become obsolete before they are ever tried. Inaction can be very expensive.

Resilient individuals are willing to experiment. They move forward into uncertain and unfamiliar territory, taking action even if the risk of failure is substantial. Rather than dot every "i" and cross every "t" before taking action, they will test their ideas, learn from experience, revise their plans, and try again.

Indicators of Experimenting

When you apply the *Experimenting* characteristic, you will tend to:
- actively engage change;
- test your ideas in practice;
- take reasonable risks; and
- try new activities.

In short, you will initiate pilot tests with innovative solutions to see if they work. You will take a leap and see what happens. If an approach doesn't pan out, you'll regroup and try something else.

For example, imagine that your company's CEO announces that the organization will be introducing new software for tracking calls with clients in the coming year. You are not very comfortable around computers, and you know that this shift will be a challenge for you. You decide to use your experimenting characteristic, so you go online and find a tutorial on the new software and get familiar with it. Then you can decide whether you will be better off learning the software and staying where you are, or beginning to plan for a job change to an environment where you will not need to work on the computer as much.

Someone with a low tendency toward experimenting might wait until the new software is introduced, go through the training, and see how their performance is affected.

How Does Experimenting Protect Your Adaptation Capacity?

Experimenting enables you to invest a small amount of your adaptation capacity to take a calculated risk. While there is a potential cost to trying out a new approach, in that you may look foolish or fail in your "trial run," you can potentially learn a great deal and prevent a high level of wasted resources later on.

Low levels of experimenting, in contrast, can lead you to proceed fairly far down an unproductive path without realizing it, with a resulting high cost if your chosen approach does not work.

Strengthening Your Experimenting

Here are five practical things you can do to improve your ability to experiment proactively:

1. Identify a small action you could take to try out a new approach to an unfamiliar situation.
2. Think about a challenging situation you are currently facing. Articulate the worst-case scenario as clearly as possible, and determine how you would prepare yourself to address each risk.
3. Team up with a friend or colleague who you see as a successful risk taker, and talk through your concerns and objections about a specific change initiative. See if you can identify how your assumptions regarding the risks differ from their perspective.
4. Try viewing a risk associated with a change initiative as a "win-win" situation—even if you are not immediately successful, what could you learn from assuming the risk?
5. Find a person who is good at experimenting and ask them to coach you.

Key #16: Try out new approaches and solutions.

> **Question for Reflection:** Which of the following seem most and least risky to you: Entering an unfamiliar social situation; trying out a new sport; expressing a new idea in writing; sharing a deeply held emotion with someone?

PART 3

Enhancing Resilience

*"We are what we repeatedly do.
Excellence, then, is not an act,
but a habit."*

—Will Durant (inspired by Aristotle)

Linda L. Hoopes

CHAPTER 17

Developing Balance

Key #17: Maintain a dynamic balance among the seven resilience characteristics.

IS IT REALLY POSSIBLE to enhance your resilience? What could you do to use your adaptation capacity more wisely in dealing with change?

Your Capacity for Resilience Development

Each person starts with their own personal baseline of resilience. Our research shows that, in addition to differences in their initial capacity, people also vary in their capacity for increasing resilience. This means you may find that you have a short or a long way to go to achieve the level of resilience you would like, and you may find the path relatively easy or hard.

Some characteristics will be easier for you to work on than others. But I believe that with consistent practice each person can increase their resilience. People can enhance their resilience by making a special effort to study and learn from those who display stronger resilience. By replicating what resilient people do, it is possible to become more resilient yourself.

You currently have some level of capacity in each of the seven resilience characteristics. In some you will have more strength; in others, less.

The key is to have a balanced portfolio of resilience skills. You will need to be able to draw on each one, and in various combinations, for dealing with changing circumstances. By having a full range of resilience skills at your disposal, you will be better prepared to cope with any contingency.

Balancing the Resilience Characteristics

Your odds of succeeding increase if you can learn to balance Positivity, Confidence, Priorities, Creativity, Connection, Structure, and Experimenting in any given situation. Being able to combine the various ingredients depending on the circumstances gives you a "resilience edge" for absorbing and adapting to change faster and better.

I believe that the resilience characteristics operate as a system to create resilient responses. That is, each characteristic plays an important role, and a very high score on one characteristic does not really compensate for a low score on another.

Think of your capabilities in each of the seven areas I have discussed as forming a profile. It probably has some highs and lows in it, although some people have strengths in all seven areas and some have significant work to do in each area. In general, I have found that a profile that is moderately high and balanced among the characteristics signals higher overall resilience than a profile that is very high in some areas and low in others.

Having a balanced profile does not mean that you are using all of the characteristics equally all of the time. Rather, it means that you can draw on your various strengths according to the demands of the situation. Since each change represents a unique set of circumstances, you are better prepared to handle a wider variety of potential changes.

A person with a less balanced profile may tend to over-rely on their strongest, most-preferred characteristics, finding it more difficult to call forth the others. Though a person with unbalanced strengths may respond well in some cases (situations where the demands match their preferred approaches), they may waste resources by not applying other skills when needed.

For example, I have observed a number of people with a very high Experimenting characteristic and a very low Priorities characteristic. These people often end up spending so much time chasing new opportunities that they never really establish a clear focus. As a result, they end up spinning their wheels in a variety of directions, going nowhere fast.

Strength in one trait does not compensate for weakness in another. I believe it is much better in the long run to have a balanced profile of capacities.

Resilience can be compared to your diet. Having three balanced meals a day is much healthier than skipping breakfast, grabbing a quick lunch, and overeating at dinner. Having a good balance of resilience scores produces a more resilient person overall.

Some Guidelines for Understanding Balance in Resilience

People seem to use their resilience characteristics in a fluid process. If we were to view them over time, they would display a varying blend of characteristics in response to specific situations. To understand this better, let's look at several guidelines for understanding balance of the characteristics:

Guideline #1: Your Resilience Depends on the Situation

Each specific change situation presents a particular set of demands. In any given change, an individual is more resilient if they can meet these demands by readily drawing on the appropriate resilience characteristics.

Not every situation calls on a person to display every characteristic. The characteristics that are important may differ from setting to setting. Since we can never be sure what a situation will demand, the person with the capability to draw on all characteristics smoothly and automatically has the greatest chance of success.

Guideline #2: Consistency is Best

A person who has equal or nearly equal strengths in all seven characteristics will probably be more resilient, in general, than someone with peaks and valleys in their capabilities. This person will be more successful in changing circumstances and across many different environments than a person with a less balanced resilience portfolio, because they can draw on each characteristic with equal ease and don't tend to over- or under-rely on certain characteristics.

Guideline #3: Guard Against Overusing Your Strengths

If you have a great deal of capability in one characteristic compared to the others, it is a strength, but you may tend to overuse this trait and underuse the others.

For example, if you have a very high *Priorities* capability, but a substantially lower *Creativity* capability, you might develop "tunnel vision," losing sight of possible alternate paths to reach desired goals.

Guideline #4: Work on Strengthening Your Weaknesses

Any capability that is extremely low indicates a tendency to underuse that particular characteristic. Low capability in any area suggests a missing piece of the puzzle. If you are not strong in a particular characteristic, you probably lack confidence in that skill and rarely use it, relying instead on the remaining characteristics.

If you have low capabilities in several areas, it means there are multiple tools that you may fail to use when change is encountered. Your response options become even more limited and restricted.

Static vs. Dynamic Balance

Because change presents continually shifting possibilities, it's impossible to face it with a fixed set of approaches. We need to be continually moving, revising, and adjusting our approach.

Our approach to change must be one of "dynamic balance"—we can only see it in motion. There is a paradox hidden in this idea. As I discussed in the early chapters of this book, people seek a sense of control and equilibrium in life. The desire to increase resilience is, in part, a desire to feel a greater sense of equilibrium during change. But because of the nature of change, the only stability that is possible occurs as a result of constant movement. A sense of equilibrium from a "dynamic balance" that is constantly shifting is as close as we can come to stability.

Equilibrium doesn't reside on calm waters where you'd expect it to; instead, the balance you are looking for is embedded in the whitewater of the turmoil you try to avoid. And the currents are constantly shifting. Moments of equilibrium can be quickly disrupted by a sudden change of events. The shelf life for the point of balance is always short-lived.

Key #17: Maintain a dynamic balance among the seven resilience characteristics.

Questions for Reflection: Which of the characteristics do you tend to overuse? To underuse? What would balance look like for you?

Linda L. Hoopes

CHAPTER 18

Building a Resilience Development Plan

Key #18: Create a resilience development plan.

Investing Your Energy

YOU CAN BECOME MORE RESILIENT over time. But you need to work at it. You need to make a personal commitment to develop yourself if you are sincerely interested in strengthening one or more of the resilience characteristics.

It will not come easily or quickly. It's not about making quick fixes, waving a wand, and "poof"—you become more resilient. As a comparison, think about improving your health. You don't become healthier by watching a show about exercise or reading a book on nutrition—you become healthier by making daily choices about what you eat and what physical activities you pursue. Just as increasing physical health involves changing daily habits, increasing resilience involves changing mental habits.

Becoming more resilient is a process that occurs over time. It requires an investment of energy in increasing knowledge, deepening your self-awareness, seeking feedback from others, and trying new approaches. It requires consistency, focus, and discipline.

Becoming a more resilient person is a major personal change initiative, and you will experience all the feelings, resistance, and dynamics that you do with other changes. You will have to leave your "comfort zone." You will have to leave some old habits behind and develop some new habits—new ways of thinking, new questions to ask, new ways of acting and responding.

This means you will have to invest some psychological resources, take a good hard look at yourself, and devote both mental and emotional energy to the pursuit of greater resilience. However, the return on your investment can be very high. The payoff is significant—higher personal productivity, faster adaptation to change, more creative approaches, and an all-around more satisfying life in the long run.

Improve Your Knowledge and Awareness

Your goal should be to move from a position of "unconscious incompetence" to one of "conscious competence." Or, said another way, you must go from "*not* knowing what you *don't* know" to "knowing what you know, and knowing how to use it."

There are any number of things you can do to improve your awareness and understanding of resilience. Reading this book will help. You can also do the following:
- Find additional resources (books, videos, courses) related to one or more of the resilience characteristics.
- Observe others who use a particular characteristic well and ask them about it.
- Practice, practice, practice.

Get Input and Feedback from Others

An important avenue for developing your resilience is to solicit opinions, perceptions, and comments from other people. In most cases, others will see you somewhat differently than you see yourself. These insights are extremely valuable for you to get a more objective, three-dimensional view of your behavior.

Some common ways to solicit feedback and input from others include the following:

- Simply ask them how *Creative* or *Experimenting* they thought you were during a recent change, and then really listen to their answers without commenting.
- Ask someone to fill out *The Quick Self-Assessment* in Chapter 9 on you, and then get them to tell you why they gave you the scores they did.
- Do a more formal 360° assessment of your resilience characteristics, soliciting feedback from your manager, teammates, subordinates, associates, customers, and/or spouse.

Coaching Can Help

Consider using a coach to help you improve your resilience. A coach can be a valuable source of know-how and tips for improving your performance.

Your coach might be someone within your organization whom you trust and who demonstrates resilience themself. This person may be your manager, a co-worker, or someone outside of your department. The key is to find someone who is both willing and able to observe your work and give you constructive feedback with resilience in mind.

Another option is to consider engaging a professional coach to help you become more resilient—perhaps a business coach or a life coach with expertise in this area. A coach can help you develop discipline and accountability to keep you on track. As you work, you may find that some of the characteristics involve deeply rooted beliefs or feelings that need some serious digging into to bring them to the surface. For example, to move from a negative to positive view of yourself may require a more in-depth examination of some of your core beliefs, past experiences, and deeply held values. In these cases, you may wish to seek counseling from a professional therapist.

Experiment

Finally, try experimenting with some new ways of thinking and acting in new situations. I've identified five concrete things you can do for each of the seven facets of resilience. Try several of them, or think up your own.

The important point is to be proactive by focusing on some specific actions you can take to improve your resilience capabilities.

Build a Plan

This chapter has provided a number of ideas for increasing your resilience. My recommendation is that you don't try to do everything at once. Pick a single characteristic to focus on first; once you've made some progress, you can add another one and build up from there. As you create your plan, I suggest that you consider the following points:

- Which characteristic do you want to work on first? (If you can't decide, I recommend that you start with Positivity or Confidence).
- What specific behaviors would you like to do more of?
- What specific behaviors would you like to do less of?

- What is the payoff to you of strengthening this characteristic?
- How will you remind yourself to change your behavior?
- How will you reward yourself for changing your behavior?
- What will you say or do to keep yourself on track when you hit "informed pessimism"?
- Who can serve as a coach or mentor for you?
- What kind of agreement will you make with this person?
- How will you evaluate your results?

Now put your plan into action, and watch the results materialize.

Key #18: Create a resilience development plan.

Question for Reflection: Working on increasing your resilience represents a change in your life. How can you use each resilience characteristic to help you build and stick to your plan?

CHAPTER 19

Resilient Teams

Key #19: When working in a team, use the power of synergy to leverage individual resilience characteristics.

Working Together to Get Things Done

IF YOU ARE LIKE MOST OF US, you probably work in a team of some kind—a management team, a project team, a consulting team, a professional team, a self-managing work team, and/or a family team. Effective team performance is a key ingredient of your personal productivity and success.

Research has shown that to be effective, teams must combine many factors—common goals, clear roles, the right skill mix, and effective processes for getting things done and working together.

Team Resilience Foundation Factors

I believe that a team's ability to maximize its performance during change also depends on the team's resilience—its collective ability to absorb change with minimum disruption and dysfunctional behavior. In other words, a resilient team optimizes its available energy and assimilation resources.

A team's resilience is not just the personal resilience of each of its members. Instead, it combines two factors—the individual resilience of each member and the collective synergy of the group. They are the two links in this chain, and both are essential.

Each member of the team possesses a specific mix of the seven resilience characteristics. Often these counterbalance one another. For instance, one member may rely on the *Priorities* and *Structure* characteristics, while another might excel in *Creativity* and *Experimenting*.

How well a team uses its unique mix of skills depends on the level of *synergy*—effective processes for combining skills and talents—among the group. A high degree of synergy allows the team to leverage its members' strengths and compensate for their weaknesses.

For example, although not every team member may be highly creative, a synergistic team can draw from the team's most creative members when needed to maximize its performance in specific situations. Applied consistently, synergy leverages the team's resilience resources to produce solutions that are better than and different from the initial ideas of individual members.

Let's explore both elements—combining a group of resilient members and creating synergy within the team—in more detail.

Combining a Group of Resilient Members

In ideal circumstances, each team member would be extremely resilient at an individual level, with balanced strengths on all of the characteristics. However, in real life, most people do not possess a perfect balance of all seven characteristics.

As a result, we need to think of balance from a second point of view. A resilient team can also achieve balance by combining members of differing strengths. A dynamic balance can be created if the team can draw on the characteristics it needs in any given situation from the team members who are strongest in those areas. In this way, the weakness of any one member is offset by the interaction of the group, and the team can be more resilient than any one of its members.

Not every group can recognize and effectively use its members' strengths. The way the group operates—how people relate to each other, communicate with one another, and value one another—has a large influence on its ability to build on its assets. This leads us to the second element of a resilient team—synergy.

Creating Synergy

Synergy is defined as the creation of an outcome that is greater than the sum of the inputs used to achieve it. What does it take to get there?

Before synergy can be achieved, two prerequisites must be in place—willingness and ability. When people share common goals and recognize that they are interdependent and must work together collaboratively, they are motivated (willing) to engage in teamwork. When team members are seen as valued and influential by peers and team leaders, and operate in an environment where their input is actively sought, they are able to bring their strengths to the group.

Once the prerequisites are in place, the work of synergistic interaction begins. This requires four steps:
1. surfacing the diverse perspectives and strengths of team members;

2. valuing and appreciatively understanding the various points of view;
3. combining the team's resources to create powerful ideas; and
4. effectively putting the team's plans into action.

People bring all kinds of resources into their team settings. If a team can recognize and use its resilience strengths as effectively as it uses other knowledge and skills, it lays the groundwork for outstanding performance when the team encounters major change.

Team Resilience Characteristics

When personal resilience and synergy are combined, the outcome is a team that operates extremely effectively during disruptive change. We can take the original set of resilience characteristics and use them to describe a team rather than an individual:

- **Positivity:** A resilient team is enthusiastic and optimistic about the opportunities that are present in the challenges it faces.
- **Confidence:** A resilient team is confident about its combined capabilities to succeed in the face of turbulence and disruption.
- **Priorities:** A resilient team aligns the objectives of individual members around a shared set of goals, and uses this sense of clarity to ensure they are using their time and energy wisely.
- **Creativity:** A resilient team incorporates multiple perspectives into its thinking, generating a broad range of possibilities and options for addressing challenges.

- **Connection:** A resilient team encourages people to support one another, reach out for assistance and input, and work collaboratively to achieve results.
- **Structure:** A resilient team incorporates effective systems, processes, and attention to detail into decision-making, planning, and other activities to ensure that everyone's energy is used most efficiently.
- **Experimenting:** A resilient team engages action in the face of ambiguity, even when risk is involved, rather than waiting for stability, and incorporates its learning into future actions.

By combining personal resilience and synergy, a team can create a combined resilience capability that allows it to significantly enhance its performance during change.

Your Challenge

If you work in a team, your challenge is twofold. First, you must develop your own personal resilience so that you can add more value to the team in a wider variety of circumstances. Second, you must take responsibility for helping your team work together in ways that optimize its skills and resources.

By increasing your own resilience and building your team's synergy, you can help lead your team to higher levels of both productivity and satisfaction.

Key #19: When working in a team, use the power of synergy to leverage individual resilience characteristics.

> **Question for Reflection:** If you are currently on a team, what actions can you take to increase the team's resilience?

Linda L. Hoopes

CHAPTER 20

Working in a Nimble Organization

Key #20: Work in a nimble organization if you can, and help make the one you are in more nimble.

The Accelerating Pace of Change

IF YOU WORK IN AN ORGANIZATION, you are no doubt feeling the stresses, strains, and pressure of ongoing change at all levels. New market development, new customers, new product introductions, new information systems, mergers, reorganizations, new leadership, cultural shifts, new programs—the list goes on to create a never-ending web of change. Surviving, much less thriving, amidst constant turbulence is getting harder and harder.

Some foresighted organizations are beginning to recognize the problem and are trying to do something about it. They can see that continuous change is draining their time and resources, and that many people at all levels are burning out, dropping out, or giving up as a result.

One thing they are not doing is slowing down the pace of change. In fact, just the opposite is occurring—the new norm is more change, at a faster pace, with more complexity.

Organizations are learning how to cope better by responding faster, absorbing change more quickly, adjusting better, and working smarter. They are learning to become more nimble organizations.

Andy Grove, the former chairman of Intel Corporation, put it this way: "You have no choice but to operate in a world shaped by globalization and the information revolution. There are two options: Adapt or die. You need to plan the way a fire department plans. It cannot anticipate fires, so it has to shape a flexible organization that is capable of responding to unpredictable events."

What does this mean, and how do you fit in the game? It means that if you want to be in an environment that supports, values, and enhances your own resilience, you need to make sure you're working in a nimble organization.

What Makes an Organization Nimble?

Nimbleness is the ability of an organization to consistently succeed in unpredictable, contested environments by implementing change more efficiently and effectively than its competitors. Nimbleness means more than just flexibility. It is a term that conveys speed, grace, dexterity, and resourcefulness, and it represents a significant competitive advantage.

Nimble companies treat their ability to manage the unexpected as a strategic asset.

How do you know if you are working for a nimble organization? Look around you. In nimble organizations:

- people operate in flexible roles that may shift on a periodic basis;
- teams tend to be cross-functional;
- decisions are made quickly;
- shifting priorities are normal;

- everyone engages in uninhibited dialogue, direct feedback, and constructive conflict;
- management is held accountable for the quality of its decisions and implementation plans; and
- you feel valued for your current performance, not how long you've been at the company.

The more of these indicators you can say "yes" to, the more nimble your organization tends to be. Now let's look at some of the important characteristics that distinguish the nimble organization from its more rigid counterpart.

How Does Nimbleness Support Resilience?

Nimble organizations tend to be populated with resilient people. Employees typically are resourceful, multi-skilled, highly motivated people who have a high tolerance for ambiguity, a desire to experiment, a willingness to appropriately challenge authority, and a focus on the success of the entire enterprise.

When an organization creates a critical mass of people with these qualities, its ability to adapt to shifting demands accelerates dramatically. People use their energy to solve problems and create solutions rather than falling prey to dysfunctional behavior.

Nimble organizations recognize the value of resilience. They insist, first of all, that leaders display resilience themselves, serving as role models for the rest of the enterprise. When leaders are hired, resilience is taken into account as a criterion that is every bit as important as the type of work experience that candidates bring to the table.

Our research has found, however, that highly resilient leaders without an equal level of resilience capability in the rest of the organization can pose a substantial problem. In this situation, leaders can easily burn out the rest of the organization, failing to recognize that the changes they are initiating far exceed the organization's absorption capacity.

So nimble organizations do more. They ensure that resilience is addressed in hiring, developing, and retaining people throughout the organization. They provide training to enhance resilience, coach for resilience, reward for resilience, and ensure that teams are maximizing their resilience.

What Does This Mean for You?

If you are seeking to develop your own effectiveness during change, your best strategy is to find an organization that actively values and supports resilience. Whether it uses the terminology presented here or not, you can learn a lot about what an organization cares about by looking at its communications, talking to people who work there, and understanding what kind of people they want to hire.

Look for clues that the organization is focused on opportunities more than on dangers (*Positivity*). Make sure the organization invests in helping people develop their strengths and capabilities (*Confidence*). See if you can figure out whether the organization has a clear sense of purpose that aligns with yours (*Priorities*). Find out if the organization is supportive of multiple ways of thinking and approaching challenges (*Creativity*) and works to create a sense of community and mutual assistance among its members (*Connection*). Try to learn about the effectiveness of the organization's processes and systems (*Structure*). And, finally, seek to understand whether the organization is open to trying new things and appropriate risk-taking (*Experimenting*) or is highly risk-averse.

This information can give you important signals about the level of support you will find for your own resilience-development efforts.

If your organization is not as nimble and resilience-supportive as you would like it to be, take action.

Strategies for Leaders

Whether you are a formal or informal leader, there are a variety of things you can do to support and build nimbleness into the organization:

- Clearly communicate a guiding vision.
- Lead by example in displaying personal resilience.
- Master the change process with all of its nuances.
- Promote resilience in the teams you work with.
- Build resilience into the organization by hiring, coaching, and rewarding resilient performers.

A nimble culture is built slowly over time through the accumulation of a thousand smaller decisions and actions. And if you don't do it, it won't happen.

Strategies for the Individual

As an employee, you are the most important building block of a nimble organization. To be nimble, an organization must be made up of resilient individuals, working together on resilient teams, under the guidance of resilient leaders.

Here are several essential things that you can do to support resilience in your organization:

- Become "consciously competent" about resilience—learn more and become an expert.
- Practice personal resilience on a daily basis—bring *Positivity, Confidence, Priorities, Creativity, Connection,*

Structure, and *Experimenting* to the large and small changes and other challenges you encounter.
- Figure out what it takes to have a relationship with your manager in which you are seen as valued and influential, and use your influence to promote effective approaches to change.
- Support resilience in the teams you are a part of and in the people you work with.
- Become an advocate for building more resilience into the organization. Highlight the need, communicate the benefits, and show others what they can do to develop nimbleness.

Organizations only become nimble when there is a critical mass of resilient leaders, teams, and individuals working together in complementary ways.

Key #20: Work in a nimble organization if you can, and help make the one you are in more nimble.

> **Questions for Reflection:** You probably belong to several organizations or groups, including your workplace, your community, and your family. Which of them appears to be the most nimble? What makes it so?

Living a Resilient Life

Key #21: Take resilience with you wherever you go.

LIVING A RESILIENT LIFE means practicing resilience in all aspects of your existence—your work, your personal life, your relationships, your family, your teams, and your organizations. Any disruption in one of these areas spills over into the others, and your effectiveness at managing the demands of change in one piece of your life determines, to a great extent, your overall quality of life.

Resilience Outside the Organization

You can use the ideas presented in this book in your community, your relationships, and your social and religious organizations. The resilience characteristics are just as effective in helping you cope with global events as in addressing workplace challenges. One of the most critical places to apply your knowledge of resilience is in your family and schools. The habits of mind that resilience encompasses are shaped very early. If children learn how to cope with change effectively when they are young, they have a skill that will enhance the rest of their lives.

Living in Balance

"Work-life balance" has been a focus of attention for decades, but as the pace of life continues to increase, it has taken on a new sense of importance—particularly with respect to the relationship between your work and family life. While achieving a sense of balance across the various domains of your life is important, I feel that there are two additional forms of balance to keep in mind when seeking to live a resilient life:

1. developing a balanced portfolio of the seven resilience characteristics; and
2. maintaining a dynamic balance among constantly shifting circumstances and priorities.

You are the architect of balance in your life. It is your challenge to manage it in a way that uses your limited adaptation capacity most effectively.

The Health Factor

Finally, I'd like to mention the connection between physical health and resilience. High levels of change put a heavy strain on your adaptation resources. Although we tend to talk about the emotional and mental burdens, there are also effects on your health and physical well-being. When your adaptation capacity is overtaxed, it can affect your health. Health problems, in turn, can further drain your capacity, making it even harder for you to maintain effective performance during change and potentially leading to a downward spiral of problems.

Most of the available research has concentrated on the mental and emotional aspects of resilience. However, there are also clear, direct links between resilience and physical well-being.

It is clear that healthy, physically fit people are more likely to show better psychological health as well. If you are healthy, you feel better. You tend to be more positive in general. You can focus outside of yourself and not worry about how you are feeling today. You are more inclined to be proactive and initiate activities without concerns about "saving your strength."

It is also clear that improving your physical fitness, no matter what shape you're currently in, has important psychological benefits. There are reciprocal links between exercise and resilience: Improving your physical fitness increases your energy, improving your ability to apply your Positivity, Confidence, Priorities, Creativity, Connection, Structure, and Experimenting characteristics. And, in return, strengthening the resilience characteristics increases the odds that you will have the motivation and discipline to exercise more and find creative ways to fit healthy activities into your already busy life.

Although it's well beyond the scope of this book to describe how to increase your physical well-being, the keys to good health and fitness are really pretty basic. Eat a healthy diet. Get regular aerobic, strength building, and stretching exercise. Maintain an appropriate weight. Get enough sleep. Hydrate. Take time to relax.

The hard part is making these things daily habits. You can use the resilience characteristics to help you:

- *Positivity* (It really works!)
- *Confidence* (I can do it.)
- *Priorities* (I want to be healthy at 100.)
- *Creativity* (There are a lot of different ways to do this.)
- *Connection* (I can learn from others how to do it better.)
- *Structure* (I have a daily routine.)

- *Experimenting* (I can take the first small step now!)

The good news is that everything counts and is cumulative. So the more you work on it, the better you get at it, and the more benefits you receive. You must make the commitment and investment, but the return on your investment keeps growing at a compound rate. Your health improves, your change quota increases, and your ability to bounce back from adversity enables you to live the life you truly want.

Key #21: Take resilience with you wherever you go.

Question for Reflection: How can I take the first step to increasing my resilience?

Linda L. Hoopes

The 21 Keys

WE CAN NOW ASSEMBLE the entire list of 21 keys for bouncing back, staying on top, and going with the flow of change in your life:

1. Recognize that change is here to stay.
2. Understand that loss of control is at the heart of change.
3. Understand the importance of resilience in adapting to change.
4. Know your quota for change.
5. Become more conscious of your own response to change.
6. Expect the unexpected so that you are rarely surprised that you are surprised.
7. Be ready for resistance, whether you view a change as positive or negative.
8. Know your orientation to change—danger or opportunity.
9. Understand the elements of resilience.
10. Look for the opportunities in changing situations.
11. Develop a "can-do" attitude.
12. Keep your focus on long-term goals and values.
13. Generate a wide range of possibilities to creatively address uncertainty.
14. Reach out to others for perspective and support.
15. Create systematic approaches to managing ambiguity.
16. Try out new approaches and solutions.
17. Maintain a dynamic balance among the seven resilience characteristics.
18. Create a resilience development plan.

19. When working in a team, use the power of synergy to leverage individual resilience characteristics.
20. Work in a nimble organization if you can, and help make the one you are in more nimble.
21. Take resilience with you wherever you go.

I can say with great confidence that if you become a more resilient person, you will be able to handle the changes in your life more gracefully and be a happier, more effective person throughout the course of your life.

Remember, it is not what happens to you, it's how you respond that matters. Life is going to throw you a lot of "curve balls." What you expect will happen and how you perceive what actually happens will shape how you respond. And you are in control of your expectations and perceptions.

Being able to adapt more quickly has become a core life skill. Mastering the art of change with resilience will help you live your life with more skill and finesse. You will be able to navigate through change more skillfully. You will be able to bounce back faster from setbacks. You will feel more in control and "on top of the situation" as you move through change of any kind.

These 21 keys are a distillation of the essential ingredients for being able to navigate change successfully. Each one provides a drop of wisdom. Taken together, they can create a significant shift in your approach to change. Decades of research, training, and consulting to hundreds of organizations and thousands of people all point to one central conclusion—resilience matters. It is important for individuals, for teams of people, for organizations, and for societies.

It can be a long and frustrating journey to become a more resilient person. The bad news is that your training never really stops. You will continue to be bombarded by more changes. And the better you get at adapting to them, the more disruption you will seem to get. (The reward for being able to handle challenges well is more and bigger challenges.)

The good news is that you can develop your resilience over time and become much more adept at managing the changes in your life. They won't stop coming, but you can get a lot better at anticipating, absorbing, assimilating, and adapting to changes when they do come.

Where from Here?

Okay. There you have it—21 keys for managing change with resilience. Now what?

These keys represent accumulated wisdom from three decades of research, my own experience, research findings, and battle scars from helping others navigate the turbulent waters of change.

I hope I have increased your awareness about the forces at work, how they affect you, and what you can do to adapt faster and better. The ultimate master key is to become more resilient—as a person, in your relationships, on your teams, in your organizations. How can you do that?

You now must be proactive and initiate the next phase for yourself. You have read this book and that is a good start. Here are several things you can do next to broaden your understanding and apply these skills:

- Pick one or two resilience traits that you want to improve.
- Look around and begin to notice how your colleagues, spouse, children, friends, and organizations are dealing with change.
- Learn more by rereading this book in two weeks, reading another book from our recommended reading list,

and making notes to yourself about your observations and perceptions.

It's now your move.

Linda L. Hoopes

Resilience Reading List

HERE ARE SOME BOOKS you might find helpful in strengthening your resilience. This list was compiled some time ago but contains much timeless wisdom. There are many more great books now available on resilience, and on the seven resilience characteristics. I encourage you to find those that speak to you and use them in your development.

Positivity

Cooperrider, David & Diane Whitney, *Appreciative Inquiry,* Berrett-Koehler Publishers, 2005

Seligman, Martin, *Learned Optimism: How to Change Your Mind and Your Life,* Alfred A. Knopf, 1990.

Seligman, Martin & Jane E. Gilham (Eds.), *The Science of Optimism and Hope: Research Essays in Honor of Martin E.P. Seligman* (Laws of Life Symposia Series, V.2), Templeton Foundation Press, 2000.

Snyder, C.R., *The Psychology of Hope: You Can Get There from Here,* Free Press, 1994.

Vaughn, Susan C., *Half Empty, Half Full: Understanding the Psychological Roots of Optimism,* Harvest Books, 2001.

Confidence

Branden, Nathaniel. *The Six Pillars of Self-Esteem.* Bantam Books, 1995.

Buckingham, Marcus & Donald O. Clifton. *Now, Discover Your Strengths.* Free Press, 2001.

Dweck, Carol, *Mindset,* Random House, 2007

Maxwell, John, *How Successful People Think,* Center Street, 2009

Priorities

Beck, Martha. *Finding Your Own North Star.* Crown Publishers, 2001.

Canfield, Jack & Mark Victor Hansen, Les Hewitt, *The Power of Focus,* Health Communications, 2000.

Covey, Stephen R., *The 7 Habits of Highly Effective People,* Free Press, 2004

Tracy, Brian. *Focal Point: A Proven System to Simplify Your Life, Double Your Productivity, and Achieve All Your Goals.* AMACOM, 2001.

Creativity

de Bono, Edward. *Serious Creativity: Using the Power of Lateral Thinking to Create New Ideas.* Harper Business, 1992.

Segal, Marci, *Creativity and Personality Type: Tools for Understanding and Inspiring the Many Voices of Creativity,* Telos, 2001.

Connection

Bolton, Robert. *People Skills.* Simon & Schuster, 1986.

Collins, Peggy Help Is Not A Four-Letter Word, McGraw-Hill, 2006

Gottman, John M. & Joan DeClaire, *The Relationship Cure: A Five-Step Guide for Building Better Connections with Family, Friends, and Lovers,* Crown, 2001.

Klaver, M Nora, *MAYDAY: Asking for Help in Time of Need,* Berrett-Koehler, 2007

Zachary, Lois J. *The Mentor's Guide: Facilitating Effective Learning Relationships,* Jossey-Bass, 2000.

Zaiss, Carl D. *True Partnership: Revolutionary Thinking about Relating to Others,* Berrett-Koehler, 2002.

Structure

Lewis, James P. *Project Planning, Scheduling & Control, 3rd Edition*, McGraw-Hill Professional Publishing, 2000.

Morgenstern, Julie. *Time Management from the Inside Out: The Foolproof System for Taking Control of Your Schedule and Your Life*. Henry Holt, 2000.

Silver, Susan, *Organized to Be Your Best!: Simplify and Improve How You Work*, Adams Hall, 2000.

Winston, Stephanie. *The Organized Executive: The Classic Program for Productivity: New Ways to Manage Time, People, and the Digital Office*. Warner Books, 2001.

Experimenting

Bennis, Warren and Burt Nanus. *Leaders: The Strategies for Taking Charge*. Harper & Row, 1985.

Kahneman, Daniel & Amos Tversky, *Choices, Values and Frames*, Cambridge University Press, 2000.

Sheehy, Gail. *Pathfinders*. William Morrow, 1981.

Other Books by Linda Hoopes

Hoopes, Linda L., *Prosilience: Building Your Resilience for a Turbulent World*, Dara Press, 2017

Additional Perspectives on Personal Resilience

Brooks, Robert & Sam Goldstein, *The Power of Resilience: Achieving Balance, Confidence and Personal Strength in Your Life*, McGraw-Hill, 2004

Goldsmith, Marshall, *What Got You Here Won't Get You There*, Hyperion, 2007

Reich, John W., Alex J. Zautra & John Stuart Hall, *Handbook of Adult Resilience*, Gailford Press, 2010

Reivich, Karen & Andrew Shatte, *The Resilience Factor: 7 Keys to Finding your Inner Strength and Overcoming Life's Hurdles*, Three Rivers Press, 2003

Siebert, Al, *The Resiliency Advantage: Master Change, Thrive Under Pressure and Bounce Back from Setbacks* Barrett-Koehler, 2005

Werner, Emmy E. & Ruth Smith, *Journeys from Childhood to Midlife: Risk, Resilience, and Recovery*, Cornell University Press, 2001.

Resilient Leaders

Conner, Daryl R. *Managing at the Speed of Change: How Resilient Managers Succeed and Prosper Where Others Fail.* Villard Books. 1992.

Kelly, Mark, Rob Ferguson, and George Alwon. *Mastering Team Leadership: 7 Essential Coaching Skills.* Mark Kelly Books. 2001.

Nimble Organizations

Conner, Daryl R. *Leading at the Edge of Chaos: How to Create the Nimble Organization.* John Wiley and Sons. 1998.

Parenting

Brooks, Robert and Sam Goldstein. *Raising Resilient Children.* McGraw Hill—NTC, 2001.

Joseph, Joanne M. *The Resilient Child: Preparing Today's Youth for Tomorrow's World.* Plenum Press, 1994.

About the Author

DR. LINDA HOOPES is the founder and president of Resilience Alliance, an Atlanta-based firm focused on helping individuals, teams, and organizations learn to thrive in turbulence. She works with clients in the areas of resilience, human energy sustainability, and change readiness.

Prior to founding Resilience Alliance in 2007, Linda spent seventeen years at ODR/Conner Partners, a consulting and training firm focused on the successful execution of organizational change. She is the author of *Prosilience: Building Your Resilience for a Turbulent World*, which won the 2018 EPIC award for best nonfiction book. She has built a global network of practitioners who apply the Prosilience framework and the Personal Resilience Profile assessment in coaching, training, and consulting.

Linda received her Ph.D. in Industrial/Organizational Psychology from the University of Tennessee and her AB in Psychology from Davidson College. She has served on the faculties of several institutions including Rutgers and Georgia Tech, and is licensed as a psychologist in the state of Georgia. She is also a musician, photographer, sailor, and massage therapist, and brings these influences into her work.

For More Information

Resilience Alliance
315 W. Ponce de Leon Ave., Suite 750
Decatur, GA 30030
Telephone: 404-371-1011
resiliencealliance.com

Websites

Prosilience

Building your resilience for a turbulent world
prosilience.com

Realization Institute

Helping organizations deliver results and increase well-being
realizationinstitute.com

Resilience Alliance

Tools and training for resilience practitioners
resiliencealliance.com

Made in the USA
Middletown, DE
10 July 2021